WHITE PANTIES, DEAD FRIENDS
& OTHER BITS & PIECES OF LOVE

WHITE PANTIES, DEAD FRIENDS

& OTHER BITS & PIECES OF LOVE

Bobby Byrd

CINCO PUNTOS PRESS

Cover Art © 2006 by Lee Merrill Byrd
Photograph of Steve Sprague © 2006 by Jane Sprague

Set in Vendetta
Book design: JB Bryan
Printed in the USA

First Edition
10 9 8 7 6 5 4 3 2 1

ISBN 0-938317-72-5

Library of Congress Cataloging-in-Publication Data
Byrd, Bobby, 1942-
White panties, dead friends, and other bits and pieces of love / by Bobby Byrd.— 1st ed.
    p. cm.
ISBN 0-938317-72-5
I. Title.
PS3552.Y66W47 2006
811'.54--dc22

                        2005037831

Thanks to the Lannan Foundation for their support.
And to the ladies at 701 Texas Avenue—Mary, Ligia and Rose. They are the light bearers.

Some of these poems, in different versions, have appeared in *Sin Fronteras*; *Santa Fe Broadside* on line at www.sfpoetry.org; *Borderlands, Texas Poetry Review*; an anthology in memory of Franco Beltrametti published by La Fondazione Franco Beltrametti; and probably a few other places which I have forgotten because of my lousy record keeping. Forgive me. And kudos to Longhouse, a very wise institution of entrepreneurial publishing of poetry and selling of poetry books. The proprietors, Bob and Susan Arnold, have long been supporters of my work.
                Like the dead poet said: Onward.
                What else is there, huh?

Ah, the white panties and the little bits and pieces of love
are always for Lee,
and for our children and their families—
for Susie Byrd, her husband Ed Holland,
and their children Hannah, John and Baby Ed;
for Johnny Byrd and Ailbhe Cormack-Aboud;
and for Andy Byrd, his wife Sandie,
and their children Santiago and Birdie.

Contents

White Panties

Genesis

The cops found Adam on the 5th floor.
Eve was dead.
Noah was on the telephone.

Why I am a Poet, #7

FOR CONNIE VOISINE

Well, this morning the oatmeal is simmering and I am eating a banana
waiting for another day in my life to take shape so bored
I pick up the shitty rightwing newspaper that says buried somewhere tiny
like inconsequential filler
the famous black actor Ossie Davis dropped dead yesterday at age 87
the police aren't saying how or why
although old age that forever culprit is the assumed killer,
but what it doesn't say is
I am 13 years old in 1955 Memphis playing hooky from church
where my brother and sisters and our widowed mother
are eating the body and drinking the blood of Jesus Christ our Lord
me lying in sin on the living room couch at 414 S. Prescott
in a city where it is illegal for me to go to school with black kids,
or vice versa, why, I will never know, but
Glendale 8-4938 is our phone number
it's been like that in my head 60 years now
and I am in the 7th grade at East High School
learning geometry and how to diagram sentences
but red-headed Albert Thomas teaches me the real lessons of life,
already 16 and driving cars and talking about pussy,
smoking Lucky Strike cigarettes
and pitching pennies and dimes at the bathroom wall,
proletariat Albert instinctively hating white middle-class Memphis
that stretched east into whiter and richer postwar suburbia,
Germantown it's called,
although he hated the niggers more,
that's what his father taught him, to hate the niggers,

that's what Albert said,
poor Albert, he hated his father too,
but I have gone astray in my story
because today is Sunday 50 years ago,
and I am watching a show called Omnibus
on the massive Motorola mahogany console television
with the rabbit ears on top,
a TV show doomed to capitalistic failure for its 1950s flamboyant intellectualism
and of course I already had pretensions of intellectualism
getting drunk on dreamy horny summer Friday nights
45 rpm records with the big holes dripping rhythm and blues onto the turntable
Jimmy Reed and Bobby Blue Bland and Little Richard,
God bless them all,
they saved my life I thank them I praise them,
them and cheap beer like JAX and Falstaff and Schlitz
when this handsome black man with the glimmery ironical smile
appears on the black and white TV screen
the black man announcing his name is Ossie Davis
whereupon he sits down on a wooden stool and further declares
that he is going to say a poem by Frank O'Hara,
a New York City poet who would rather be a painter than a poet
but he is not a painter, what can you do?
so I lie there on the couch in my adolescent loneliness
listening to some Sunday morning poem
Ossie Davis is telling me friendly
like
he is in my living room for the first and last time in his life
which is how this other guy Mike Goldberg,
a painter,

likewise enters,
wrapped in the landscape of that long ago poem
putting sardines in a painting,
thereby befuddling the poet Frank O'Hara
who is wondering why, why
is Mike putting those sardines inside his painting?
the poet using the voice of Ossie Davis
saying to me, Yes,
it needed something there, thus, the sardines
stupefying Frank O'Hara so much
because he is presently engaged in writing a poem about oranges,
so much orange in the world, it means so much,
the color orange,
the meaning of life almost, orange, oranges, how terrible orange is,
and life is terrible too,
so terrible that the poem grows and grows,
it's 12 poems by now and he hasn't mentioned orange yet,
maybe orangutan but not orange,
days go by,
and a gate opens in my heart wide enough
so that I understand in a little bit of an epiphany—
New York is no different from Memphis
with the days going by
hamburgers and milk shakes down at the Normal Drugstore
sardines and oranges in a New York City poem
how Frank O'Hara can finish his poem without using the word orange,
no oranges hanging juicy from a green tree in California or Florida
never once
except he titles the poem "Oranges"

and one day in a gallery he sees Mike's painting
empty of sardines except it's called "Sardines"
like it makes sense
certainly a quiet revelation
so I wander
to the bathroom to pee and then to the kitchen
for a peanut butter and mayonnaise sandwich on Rainbow bread
while Ossie gets off his wooden stool and disappears
as far as I was concerned for the next 50 years until just now,
today, my god,
oranges and sardines and
I'm sorry Ossie
I miss you and Frank O'Hara
but what about Mike Goldberg
whatever happened to him?
Is he dead?
I never saw any of his work.

The Soul of Osama bin Laden

A Very Short Novel

October 2001

logos is the shadow of what happened
—JACK COLLOM, "ARGUING WITH SOMETHING PLATO SAID"

1.

The day began with October darkness and wind blowing dust
through all the cracks in the house. A train was moaning, going
someplace else, anyplace else. I turned on the radio. National Public
Radio was announcing that Osama bin Laden's soul, tainted and
crippled by fundamentalism, had escaped her master's body. A woman
reporter in Baghdad was stating that the tall bearded Arab with
obsessed eyes had announced the news on a video tape broadcast by
the Al Jazeera network. The leader of the al-Qaeda brotherhood did
not seem to care. He believes he is doing the work of God, and he
suffers no doubt. Now, without his soul to plant confusion, he will do
as he wishes. Prominent Muslim theologians, the reporter continued,
have theorized that Bin Laden's soul must have listened to the cries
of the dying—she must have wept, watching the souls of the dead
men and women and children become food for the moon. The moon
is always hungry for souls. Thus, the soul of Osama bin Laden escaped
the body and she became a bird. She went looking for a place that
looked to her like home.

2.

I live in El Paso, Texas, a geography that is very much like Afghanistan, and this morning the soul of Osama bin Laden arrived and sat grieving and translucent in the leaves of the bougainvillea outside my office. She had taken the shape of a mockingbird. The sun was shining. The soul of Osama bin Laden was curious how mockingbirds and sparrows and house finches could have learned the sacred dance of sex. How can birds, she wondered, be so wise?

3.

I went downtown to drink a café latte and to watch the people walk down the street. The soul of Osama bin Laden went with me. I sat at the counter in the café where I like to watch the world go by. Maggie, skinny and red-headed, took my order. Maggie is not a Muslim, and she is not a Christian. She wears her jeans so that her belly is exposed. Pale and freckled. Sexual. Her belly button was the holy place where she received nourishment from her mother. The place of beginning. The place where she can climb back down into the darkness to find her mother and to find her father. And the parents of her mother and her father. The circle that is never broken.

The soul of Osama bin Laden decided to ride on Maggie's shoulder.

4.

Art Lewis walked in. Tall, lanky and very black. He was wearing a black suit and a black shirt and shiny black shoes and a very nice black porkpie hat. Art is growing old, but nobody ever asks him how old. Maybe that's because he is a wise man. His wisdom is rooted in music.

Every day of his life Art Lewis steps into the river of his life and prays into his jazz saxophone. His sacred horn blows away the stifling air of fundamentalism. Right and wrong, innocence and guilt are notes in the same piece of music. Improvisation as a devout way of life. It's his spiritual practice.

Maggie brought Art Lewis a cup of green tea. Art, she said with a smile on her freckled face, you smell like marijuana, you better be careful. Art laughed, and gold glistened inside his mouth.

Art was wearing a long necklace of wide silver links with turquoise scattered here and there like stars. A cheap necklace really—not real silver, not real turquoise, but it was handsome hanging around Art's black neck. Art, I asked, where did you get that handsome necklace? Oh, he said, a wino in the alley outside the Cincinnati Street Bar gave it to me. The guy was an Indian from some place called Acoma. He wanted me to play him some blues. So I played him some alley blues, and he gave me the necklace.

5.

The soul of Osama bin Laden had disappeared. She had flown away to hide behind a garbage can in the alleyway of Art's story. She wanted to listen while Art played his golden horn. And she fell asleep. She dreamed she was giving birth to a child. When she opened her legs, she found a dead baby boy. Art Lewis sighed and with his horn he collected up the grief and blood and afterbirth like a priest who had given the holy sacrament. The wino understood. He mumbled prayers and chants he found unused in his heart and then he carefully buried the dead baby in the dumpster. The lid clanged shut. The alleyway, he said, smells like urine, but now it is a holy place.

6.

Art played his sacred horn, a riff he called "Bin Laden's Dead Baby Blues," a song so sad it made the wino weep. The wino wandered away looking for some sort of God. Any kind of God as long as there were no hard and fast rules. Before he left, the wino gave Art the silver and turquoise necklace. The necklace was stolen merchandise. Art didn't care. He put it around his neck and went back to playing his horn in the dark alleyway.

The soul of Osama bin Laden listened for a while more, but the moon was tugging at her. Here at the end of this story she was able to let go.

May God grant her peace.

A Visit from the Archangel Gabriel

Orthodox priests had blessed this war.
"The Turks are rising up again.
They come to take our sacred places."

The grainy footage shows a thin teenager,
his hands are tied behind his back, he steps forward in silence.
Two bursts from an automatic rifle rip open his back and he flops to the ground.
"There. That's my brother. There he is falling down there."
That's the voice of a young Muslim woman, Safeta Muhic,
She is 23 years old in this poem, a mother of two,
She is staring at her television set.
She flicks the remote from one channel to the next.
She wants another chance to see the Serbian gunmen killing her brother—
July 1995, the War in Bosnia.
The video was taken 10 years ago.
It's 12 minutes long.
The soldiers joke and laugh about their prisoners, six Muslim men.
By gunpoint they order the four youngest men into a line.
One of these young men is her brother.
They step forward, one by one, and the soldiers execute them.
The cameraman,
an artist
in the land of the forever dead,
carefully films the bullets entering each man's body.
He includes the final shots to the head.
Now the last two Muslims, the oldest of the six,
drag the dead bodies of their comrades to another building.
One asks for water.

The soldiers laugh, they aim and fire.
At first Safeta would not watch.
The video was poison, it made her sick.
Now she says she cannot help but try to see her brother's last few moments.
She is addicted to seeing him die.
There must be some scientific name for this strange disease.

Jill's Socks

Jill pulls on her thick blue socks,
the ones flecked with gold.
First the left, then the right.
She giggles—
the sock on the right foot
has a hole in the heel!
These, she says with a big smile,
are her favorite socks.
She bought them in Germany
when she and Joe
traveled to see the little town
made of ancient stone and mortar
where she was born
60 some odd years ago.
The war was going on.
Death walked the street with a moustache,
Death wore white gloves and carried a bucket of fear,
Sometimes death smelled like an old woman's perfume,
Other times death smelled like rotten meat.
Jill didn't understand.
She was a little girl playing in the loft of a barn.
Her mother was a young woman with a big smile
playing Mozart sonatas on a violin
and raising four kids in the gloom of that ugly war.
Jill's father rode a motorcycle
and was getting ready to die.
Jill doesn't want to throw away her purple socks.

Motel Room

Ozona, Texas.
Empty. Empty
As a wine bottle.

Traveling by Air

The schizophrenic woman
black curly hair square jaw
smoked her cigarette
and watched the full moon
navigate the night skies.
I said: "It's a pretty night, huh?"
She didn't answer my question.
She knitted her thick eyebrows
and puffed on her fag.
Thinking is work.
She was moving ideas around
in her head like furniture.
Furry clouds scattered like frightened dogs.
She said she sees things printed in the sky.
"The clouds tell me stories.
Like a regular storybook.
Look, there," she said, "there's an angel."
I followed her finger toward a cloud
swirling around the moon.
The night got darker.
The woman swallowed more smoke
and blew it at the sky.
The smoke was a shield to protect us.
A weapon.
She said: "I don't like angels.
They can't be trusted."

She smashed the cigarette into a dish and lit another.
She took a drag and sucked up the smoke through her nose.
She was an expert.
The fresh cigarette was like a new idea.
She relaxed. She lay back in her chair.
She said: "My mom and dad,
They're both dead.
They just went away.
I'm glad.
But lots of times I see them in the sky.
And today I saw an airplane
big enough
to pick me up and take me away.
It had windows and a toilet and everything."

Body of Christ, Texas

September 1999

A motel room for 45 bucks a night.
The American League Championship Series.
Boston ahead 2-1, bottom of the 7th.
Good.
I hate the Yanks.
I fix a martini.
Life is okay thus far.
But Knobloch doubles to left.
Score tied 2-2.
Fuck the Yanks.
There's no hope for the world.
There never was.
Then comes the knock at the door.
A skinny woman wants me to help her with her boat.
The boat sits on a trailer and the trailer is hitched to a red Trans-Am.
The car is old and beat-up.
Yellow Mexican plates.
The woman is taller than I am, wearing those black wedges on her feet.
I like tall women.
Silver toenails.
Brown hair.
Sunglasses.
Leathery brown skin from too much sun.
She lives near a Mexican beach on a street at the edge of middle age.
She wants to die before she's 50.
She has long legs, and she's so thin

I could put my fist between the flesh of her thighs.

The boat is a white speedboat.

It has two huge Mercury outboard motors perched on the stern.

She uses the boat to smuggle prophecy and other contraband

into the heart of the American Empire.

I tell her that Mercury was the messenger for the gods.

Also a thief and a capitalist.

Like a good American citizen, she says.

Like George Steinbrenner, I say.

Like the fucking Yankees.

She says I have been selected.

She says we will be going somewhere soon.

My job is to be ready.

The Day I Met Pancho Villa in the City of Angels
FOR DAVID ROMO

It was the last day of the Muslim Hajj, 2003,
the United States was at war against Terrorism,
and Homeland Security had issued an "Orange Alert"
because two years before Osama bin Laden
and the al-Qaeda Brotherhood had toppled the Towers
murdering all those people
and rattling the cage of Capitalism.
Me, I was minding the business of my life—
downtown Los Angeles, the corner of 6th and Hope,
a wonderfully clear day after rain—
when I was attacked by a beautiful woman with perfect lips.
She lobbed Arabic terrorist babble at my psyche.
I was wearing my embroidered Uzbekistani pill hat
and she mistook me for a Muslim foreigner.
Her anger frightened me, and I stumbled into the street.
She was quick to see my confusion,
and like a devious guerilla she switched to English.
She screamed that Jesus Christ was present in my life,
yes, in the here and now,
and she told me to repent and accept Him into my life.
I walked away like a guilty man
down to the Pantry Restaurant on Figueroa Street
for the fried ham and two eggs over-easy.
I don't think Mohammed or Jesus
would have been happy with my breakfast choice,
but they're dead

—May God grant them peace!—

and me, I was on the low-carb diet, trying to lose 10 more lbs,
so please help me, I prayed to them both
as I sat at the counter and discovered
two Mexican short order cooks
preaching a wordless sermon of the Dharma,
so perfect and elegant even Buddha himself
would have laid down his flower to watch.
The Pantry was packed with hungry customers,
the waiters barked intricate orders—
the cook on the left patiently flipped eggs
and fried the ham, the bacon and sausage
while he danced
like a solitary crane in the river of waiters flowing past,
and the cook on the right meditated on pancakes,
omelets and a very large pile of potatoes.
He likewise danced
as he chanted curses in Spanish
to lubricate the gears of the food chain.
That's when I saw Pancho Villa
sneering at me the gringo from two stools down.
His mouth was full of scrambled eggs and sausage,
the famous moustache white and greasy
under his beat-up Stetson hat.
He stunk of horseshit and gunpowder.
"It's true," he muttered, "I killed many thousands of men,
some who deserved it, many others who didn't.
I could have lived with that. That's what war is.

But in Santa Rosalía a bruja shot at my head.
She hated me, she and her compañeras.
Some sore burst in my heart, poisoned me.
I had those women killed for hating me.
Their petticoats fluttered like moths in the flames,
the bones of their womanhood crackled,
and the desert stunk of burning hair and flesh.
Los Dorados were disgusted with their jefe.
But that day I did not care. For so many years
I had found peace in the beds of women.
But the witches of Santa Rosalía
snuffed out the flames of my heart,
they cursed my soul with this wandering.
Now I have witnessed a terrible century of war.
Nothing has changed—the rich and the poor,
the hatred, the anger, the delusion—the cancers eat
at the holy body of humanity.
My eyes are emptied of tears.
No flowers will ever grow on my grave.
Still I am a hungry man,
hungry for justice, hungry for escape."
He looked up from his eggs and sausage.
The two cooks continued to work and to dance,
a corrida of grace and dignity.
Their hearts and bodies carried no shame.
Pancho watched.
The waiters came and went, the customers ate.
"Híjole," Pancho grunted, "they dance and they dance."
He looked over at me, sadness in his ghost eyes.

"Listen to me," he said. "Poverty and war,
they are brother and sister. They sleep in the same bed.
We are cursed with their twisted children."
Then he passed me the Tabasco Sauce.

Saturday is the Sabbath

1.

An hour ago when I was eating my lunch and reading a book,
this old guy—short and stout, but with big hands—
started pounding on the front door.
I didn't want to be bothered.
I knew it had to be another beggar, some
dirt farmer from Zacatecas looking for the New World.
I'm sorry. I wasn't in the mood.
Of course some days, mostly Saturdays,
and today is Saturday,
the Seventh Day Adventists
come knocking and wanting to save my soul.
I never want my soul to be saved.
I don't believe in souls
—my soul, his soul, your soul—
but if I did, I would want my soul
to ride on the deep ocean of my body
like an ancient sailing ship, some wild adventurer in charge,
his black beard and the night sky both
dripping with stars.

2.

Whoever it was wouldn't quit knocking.
So what was I going to do?
I opened the door and there was this old guy
shuffling around on clubfeet

stuck into sandals, you know
the kind, the tire treads—

"Me llamo Lorenzo,
me llamo Lorenzo,
me llamo Lorenzo!"—

Damn!
He was peeking at me through the screen door.
like he was writing his own play.
My part was to be the Gringo Forever,
he was going to play the Mexican,
like neither of us had no other choice
until of course
The End.

3.

I refused the part and began writing my own play.
I decided he was the club-footed god Hephaistos,
that ill-begotten Greek, the despised son of Hera,
half-brother of the fabulous Ares,
this Hephaistos a.k.a. Lorenzo,
a god tossed from Olympus
falling like a star through the skies
for light years, poor guy
who took his sadness and hid it in his heart,

only to land in Mexico and to cross the river
going North, only
to find himself on my front porch,
his big workman hands
suddenly butterflies
swirling in the air,
the same hands that fashioned elegant furniture
and jewelry of gold
for Zeus, that old fart of a God who
made love to swans
while the other specters of the sacred
dallied and drank and ate and bickered in the heavens,
never able to separate
the divine from their lust for earthly pleasure.

4.

I have the same problem.

5.

This old man—or god or Lorenzo or whatever—
said his wife was in Thomason Hospital.
The doctors had cut out her appendix.
He said it in lousy English and country Spanish and wild pantomime,
those big calloused hands cutting across his lower belly
to display the open wound.
Miraculously, he dipped the hands into the slit of his wife's belly
and plucked out the infected piece of meat.

His hands fashioned the narrative
of her suffering in the space between me and him.
A putrid smell. Yellowing flesh.
So, yes, I wanted to tell him that this morning I woke up
with the taste of my dead brother's sweat on my lips.
That all I wanted to do was write poems for my dead brother.
But my terrible Spanish and inarticulate hands
wouldn't let me go into these particulars.
Lorenzo was persistent.
He needed food for when his wife came home.
She needed to eat.
So I gave him some milk, two cans of black bean soup,
and a can of chicken noodle soup.
It was something I could do for this old man,
this bedraggled god standing
on the other side of the screen door with his sad story.
Lorenzo thanked me for the food,
but goddamn him, he wouldn't go away.

"Dinero," he said, "I want dollars también.
Limpio su alley. Soy good worker."

Again he opened up the palms of his hands.
His left hand had a large blister
that was purple with the blood underneath the skin.
In the palm of his hand, a tenuous life-line
departed the spider web of sorrow,
sliced across the fat flesh place under his thumb,
and trekked into the bleak future

that will be his everyday
in the United States of America.

5.

Gods are not allowed here.
Not on this side of the river.
Gods are terrorists of the soul.
We don't want no fucking Gods.

6.

Lorenzo's eyes were pieces of dark stone jammed into his head.
I gave in.
I said, "Sure, puede limpiar el callejón."
Lorenzo the old man didn't smile or say thank you.
"Shovel," he mumbled in his shitty English,
and he made like he was digging a hole.
He put the food I had given him on the front porch,
then he followed me around to the side of the house
where I gave him a rake and a shovel.
"Dos horas," Lorenzo said, "I work dos horas."
I said: "Okay, okay."
He ducked into the alley.
An hour has passed.
I can hear him now chopping at the weeds,
I can hear him scraping the ground with the rake.

All I have is a twenty-dollar bill.

Saying Goodbye to Ann Enriquez

It's the Sunday night three days after you died.
I keep remembering you inside your body.
Like a ghost.
Little glimpses here and there,
like running into an old friend at Albertson's—
the aisle where they stock the sandwich spreads and the jellies.
I'm supposed to pick up a jar of peanut butter,
a loaf of bread, a nice bottle of wine, one or two other things.
But you are waiting for me
gray and tired but your eyes are radiant.
Gaspar, you say, is at home, staring at a blank canvas.
He's lost, but what can you do?
You tell me the cancer simply asked you into the other room.
The bright lights of commerce tremble in your shade
and I become embarrassed—your death
was a random event, like
a drive-by shooting or a freak accident on I-10.
Our lives disappear like so much white noise.
You kiss me on the cheek and whisper goodbye.
Your lips are cold.
A woman looking for a jar of mayonnaise
pushes her cart with its load of food and a screaming kid
between us, and you are gone.
I'm left alone, sad and uncertain.
I should have had a gift for you to take on your journey.
A flower perhaps.

A Mexican woman had been outside the store
standing in the cold and selling beautiful gardenias
she had smuggled across the river.
Two dollars each and the gardenias smelled so sweet.
I should have bought you a Mexican gardenia.
Oh well.
I proceed to the checkout.
A pretty girl named Estela scans my groceries.
$27.83 worth of life's wheel.
Just the way life is, one day to the next.

White Panties

This afternoon while the hot sun
clattered through the summer sky
like a nail in search of a coffin,
I found a pair of your white panties
you had misplaced in my underwear drawer,
so simply surprising . . . oh, I couldn't help myself.
I sniffed at the panties.

Ahhh.

The panties were so clean and fresh with soap and Clorox.

We are getting old, huh?
Me and you—
almost 40 years we've slept in the same bed.
And yet there I was like a dog
sniffing at your clean white panties.

You are in Tulsa
visiting with your friends, the ones
I argue with in my head, the ones
who believe that a kingly god governs the world
and so in my lonely summery daydream
they question my devotion to your white panties.
They would tell me, I believe, to put
the white panties in your underwear drawer
where they belong.

They must have their reasons.
I have mine.

Outside the window despite the heat
our cat and a mockingbird were playing their game
to decide who will live the longest.
The cat was lying serenely in the thick green grass.
He waved his white-tipped tail as a flag
to entice the mockingbird to dive closer and closer.
The bird pretended she didn't understand.
She squawked in defiance at the cat's claws.
You and I know that the mockingbird will lose the game.
Already this summer we've found the feathers
of three mockingbirds scattered in the green lawn.

        But I want to write a love poem for you.
     This parable of the cat and the mockingbird
has intruded somehow into what I want to say.

Please let me try again.

I want to tell you that
I truly want to forgive your friends in Tulsa.
And likewise
I am trying to forgive myself for the anger
that I carry in my heart like dirty laundry.
I tell myself, We are who we are.
Nothing special.
Thank God our bodies can become such innocent travelers.

Any time of the day our bodies will forgive us
suddenly like . . .

                    like hummingbirds buzzing our ears
            like unexpected desert smells
    yes, like rain
like that night last week

the night before you left,
little bits of trash muddying my love for you,
but when I climbed into bed beside you
my heart miraculously becoming clean and fresh,

        like

your white panties misplaced in my underwear drawer—

   Oh, my love,

   your panties are the sails of a womanly ship
   afloat in a holy but dangerous sea.
   The ship is sailing to the end of the world,
   and I am waiting for you to come home to me.

Life after 60

It's like a war now,
Us against the Angels—
Kapow!
They got Herbie.
Shot him through the heart.
He didn't have a chance.

The Hospice Poems

IN MEMORY OF STEVE SPRAGUE

Hospice—1. *A shelter or lodging for travelers, pilgrims, foundlings, or the destitute, especially one maintained by a monastic order.* 2. *A program that provides palliative care and attends to the emotional and spiritual needs of terminally ill patients at an inpatient facility or at the patient's home.*

The birds have vanished into the sky
And now the last cloud drains away.

We sit together, the mountains and me,
Until only the mountain remains.

LI PO
8th Century
TRANSLATED BY SAM HAMILL

Steve,

It's nice to watch all these women
dancing around you, taking care of you
like lovers at a Dionysian feast.

You are the King, the summer is hot.

I don't know if you understand
what is happening in your house.
We are all here to wait for your death.

Steve,

You have become another Ishmael,
the ship has sunk,
Ahab that bastard is dead
and you are riding a handmade coffin
on the wide green sea.
But, unlike Ishmael,
you cannot tell us your story;
nor are you ready to let go
and simply sink deep into the ocean
clothing your raggedy body
in emptiness.
You breathe and sweat and gasp for breath,
and Jane and Edna and the rest of us
rub your body and wonder
without making the words aloud
if you are inside.

Steve,

Edna is angry.
She's angry at you for going off to die.
She's angry at God
for dragging her father down inside that hole.
That's what she keeps saying.
The telephone call.
You and Jane were still in Shanghai.
And Edna was getting ready to come save you.
She was going to be Wonder Woman.
You told her to look in the bottom of the hole.
That's where you were—"At the bottom of a hole."
Those are the last real words you spoke to her.
Months ago.
And she couldn't save you.
Wonder Woman couldn't save you.
She has only one real eye inside her skull.
The other eye is dead, a glass eye
made of holy magic.
When she was a kid, Wonder Woman,
to the amazement of her friends,
would pull the magic eye out of its socket
and roll it along the hardwood floor.
Wonder Woman's magic eye
was going to find her father
in the bottom of that empty hole.

Steve,

I'm in El Paso and I can't sleep.
Since December sleep is all you do.
You are not in paradise.
You are not inside Plato's cave.
At least you are at home again,
No more machines blinking and beeping—
Beelzebub's electric angels
sweeping away our stories and myths
like so much garbage.
I want to cry but I can't cry.
I want to find the Buddha on the road and kill him.
Likewise Jesus Christ.
That can be my gift to you
in your dying,
a pile of dead and rotting gods
littering the Albuquerque morning
like so much white noise.
Outside my window the blue dawn
is staining the black sky. Soon
the moon will disappear
into the daylight. I will go to work
and forget all about you for a while.
I pray that Jane has slept
a good night's sleep.

Steve,

I want to quit drinking but I can't.
It's become a "thing."
You understand that, huh?
Although you probably
no longer care
about my dilemmas.
Everything is vanity,
the Preacher Man said,
vanity and striving
after the winds that blow
down from the mountains.
But my drinking . . .
Like an old raggedy sweater
my mother gave me
when I was growing up.
13 years old.
It smelled like Memphis dirt.
I loved that sweater.
I had good times inside that sweater.
Scary shit too.
Dead people.
Rollicking laughter.
Broken cars.
Forgotten promises.
Bo Diddley was a man.
It was serious shit.
And you're in that hospital bed

Fifty years later
waiting for the Angel of Death.
I can't quit my drinking.
Not yet.

Steve,

Outside your big window is sunshine,
hummingbirds, a family of roadrunners
going back and forth, house sparrows
and finches. I also spotted some kind
of yellow bellied warbler in the tree.
Tomorrow the caregivers quit feeding you.
Jane has said it's time to say goodbye.

Steve,

Your body is a bag of bones.
Your flesh is not warmed by desire.
These damn biofeedback devices
record the last few days
of your life, an oxygen tube leads
to the hole some nameless doctor
sliced into your trachea,
a feeding hose sticks out of your belly
so the caregivers can pour
water and liquid food
directly into your intestines.
The food never has to pass GO.
You are GO, Steve, you are IT.
I pray everyday that you are
somewhere inside riding
the raft of your body
into the sea of formlessness
and some complete moment
of enlightenment.

Are you there, Steve?
Steve, are you there?

Steve,

I bought a bottle of delicious red wine,
but it's been untouched.
Your dying is our drunkenness.

Steve,

I am eating Lee's chicken soup.
She made a great big pot for everybody—
celery and carrots and gooey thick broth.
When I eat chicken soup,
I daydream about making love.
You would understand perfectly.

Steve,

The bearded guy who replenished
your supply of oxygen
had the radio in his big truck
tuned to the *Rush Limbaugh Show*.
That fat asshole was bitching about
white guy romantic liberals
like me and you. But other than that
the bearded guy seemed okay—
a wife and three kids at home,
he did his job professionally,
and he wore an old style
Pittsburgh Pirates baseball cap.

Steve,

This morning the lost poets
of the ancient Upanishads
bore witness to a holy presence
inside each of us they called
the Golden God, the Self,
the Immortal Swan,
and then three roadrunners
walked across
the adobe wall in your yard.

Steve,

At the food co-op the clerk named Alice
asked about you and Jane, your
suffering, Jane's grieving.
I didn't know what to say.
I was confused.
I mumbled something or other,
embarrassed, said you were dying
and handed her my credit card. Alice
gave me that sad look of commiseration
that Jane must endure everywhere she goes.
Alice and I waited together for my card
to be blessed—our little communion.
Then she went on to the next customer,
a handsome grey-haired guy about our age.
He was buying almonds, eggs, vitamin C
and a hot cup of jasmine tea.

Steve,

Lee and I drove home—
Albuquerque to El Paso—
250 miles in three and a half hours.
Lee went straight to bed, and I got drunk.
We didn't want to talk to each other.
We were afraid to talk to each other.
So I sat on the front porch stoop,
(Miles Davis playing *Kind of Blue*)
and watched the waxing summer moon.
Remember the Colorado moon?—
me and you sitting by the Rio Grande
watching the beaver swirl the darkness.
We were not even thirty back then.
And now we are old men,
Me this sort of fat white guy,
listening to Miles play his magic horn
from the black side of Paradise
while I write silly letters to you
to keep me busy as you die.

Steve,

You'll be dead soon.
Maybe a week, maybe sooner.
The pancreas and the kidneys
will shut down first, your
urine will turn almost black.
Etcetera.
You know me.
I get sick listening to the rules of God.
Jane called, said they put you in a sling
and took you outside
among the hummingbirds—
Jane and that remarkable coterie of caregivers,
mostly women, of course.
They make up sacred ceremony as they go along,
an improvisational and holy dance
of chatter and hands trying to crack open
your body for a last glimpse at your soul.
The women are so beautiful.
No wonder we were so horny
all these many years.

Steve,

Your mother stands by your bed.
Ninety-three years old,
she looks at you
her youngest son
and weeps.
She is an ancient white crane
standing deep in the cold river
that rushes by toward the sea.
The white crane that your mother
has become no longer fishes.
She is not hungry for food.
Nor is she thirsty.
Her true desire
is to flap her wings
one last time—she wants
you and her
to soar away to the other shore.

Steve,

Every morning Jane
attends to her rituals
of whispering in your ear
and brewing the coffee.
She caresses your face
and massages your limp hand,
she prepares herself.
She does not blame you,
and her work every day is
not to blame herself.
The yellow tulips
she arranges in a vase
by your bed are mortal.

> *I love you.*
> *I love you not.*
> *I love you.*
> *I love you.*

Jane drinks a glass of wine with dinner.
Maybe two.
At the evening reading around your bed
a guest reads a canticle by St. Francis de Assisi—

> *Be praised, my Lord,*
> > *for our sister, bodily death*
> *from whom no living thing can escape.*

Blessed are those whom she finds
doing your most holy will
for the second death cannot harm them.

Jane asks her friends
to leave her alone with you.
She washes your private
places, your genitalia
and your asshole. She speaks
words to you—words of
confusion and despair,
words of love.
She hopes you hear
and that you understand.
She kisses you good night
and wishes you well
on your journey of sleep.
But if you should die before
she wakes, she prays
to God your soul to keep.

Steve,

When we got home from Albuquerque,
here's what happened—first,
Juan Hernandez, our janitor,
the Mexican guy who crosses
into the United States every morning
so he can work for us,
the guy that we put so much trust in,
. . . well, he broke into the cash drawer
and stole $100 or so.
Lee and I were heartbroken.
Then son-in-law Eddie
reminded me
that our business is on the rocks.
Bankruptcy is a real possibility.
So that night I saw Randy Johnson—
winner of 5 Cy Young Awards,
sure-fire Hall of Famer,
throws the fastball at 100 mph,
6-foot 10 and ugly as burnt shit—
pitch for the El Paso Diablos
doing rehabilitation
against the Midland Rock Hounds.
I mean, the Big Unit is scary.
Period.
He's rehabbing his busted up knee,
so he needed some Double-A Ball
to get ready for the Bigs.

He struck out 5 of the first 6,
then in the 3rd and 4th innings
he started hitting batters,
   WHOMP, a guy in the shoulder;
      WHOMP, a guy in the thigh . . .
And then Number 33 dropped his bat,
turned around as if to run away
and got Randy's fastball
right between the shoulder blades.
   WHACK.
I laughed and laughed, laughed
like a crazy man, laughed
so hard I wanted to cry
for you.

Steve,

It's 5:30 in the morning,
Friday, July 25, 2003.
Edna called with the news.
that you are dead now.
Been dead four hours.
What's that like
on the other side, huh?
I went outside to look
at the dark blue morning,
feeling an emptiness.
Lee went for a walk.
She wanted time alone
to think and pray for you.
The blue morning
gave me back nothing
except my breath.
Your slow dying has made
me remember
that the breath of my body
is sacred.
Steve, I don't know how
to pray for the dead.
I miss you already.
The mountains are only
mountains, the sun is
but a morning star.
Goodbye.

Death is slow but death is sure
Halleloo, halleloo

Death is slow but death is sure
Halleloo, halleloo

Death is slow but death is sure
When death come somebody must go

And we must have that true religion
Halleloo, halleloo

—A TRADITIONAL GOSPEL
AS SUNG BY LEADBELLY

Other Bits & Pieces of Love

This Morning in Our Bed

Monday, July 29, 2002. Yesterday the news was all about the nine miners in Somerset, PA, that were trapped deep in the earth for 77 hours before being rescued. They had tethered themselves together because, in the event they died, they would all be found.

This morning the summery feathery breeze
licks at the hair of my naked legs. Outside
the window I see a blossom on your red hibiscus
shimmering and bending, the leaves
rich and green like money.
Money.
We have never been much good with money.
Here we are at the front door of old age
and we don't have much money to count as our own.
I do have that new book of poems
where Cold Mountain and his buddy Pickup
are sticking out their tongues and laughing at us.
Pigeons are cooing on the roof of the house next door
where our daughter lives.
We're so lucky to have our grandchildren next door.
Life is very simple, Cold Mountain says.
Sometimes the miners climb out of the cave.
Sometimes they die in the cave.
Cold Mountain doesn't cut us any slack, huh?
Down the street dogs are barking at each other.
A hummingbird sucks at the sugar water.

Jacob's Ladder is a Tree that Grows out of the Earth

December 2003

—FOR JOHN BYRD, WHO WAS WITH ME AT THE TIME

This all happened
somehow like this
exactly
and I will write love poems until I die.

Always childhood gun dreams stay too close to my heart
like the tortured prisoners of Abu Ghraib
naked in the face of Allah
under the face of the moon
forced at gun point and snarling dogs
into un-Godly deeds of disgrace
reported in the passive sentences of America . . .

prisoners anally penetrated by phosphorous tipped nightsticks
prisoners fondled by female guards
prisoners fed from toilets
prisoners ridden like dogs
prisoners forced to eat pork and drink liquor . . .

one prisoner naked and smeared with mud or feces
arms extended
ankles cuffed and crossed
standing like Christ on the Cross

thus mocking the path of holiness
with

a pornography of violence
the full moon of May in Baghdad
or may not
caressing my own anger
my mother is dead
Hush, Bobby, hush now,
East 96th Street New York City
where that same orangey Baghdad moon rising
fleshy and rosy
startles me
into sudden forgiveness
mysterious Central Park autumn blossoms
falling as memory
already softening up my heart
so I raise my arms in surrender
lie down in that grassy field
I am ready to talk
to ask for mercy and forgiveness
to sit quiet
to spill the beans
to tell everything to the faithful enemy
of my separateness
the world is too full for my words
hearts and blossoms drifting fresh and pure
in the shit and grime.

The Moon is the Eye of A Crow
A Grandfather Poem just a Few Days before Winter Solstice

It's the time of winter solstice, and the light
disappears so quickly.
Already the sun begins to fall behind the mountain.
I put my grandson in his backpack, and we go up toward that mountain.
At our backs the twilight full moon
freshly rising
is the yellow eye of a giant crow.

Thank you, Crow.

Every morning and evening I take my blood pressure,
and all day I attend to the thumping of my heart.
Time has passed by my window like an old girlfriend
who lives in New York City on 26th Street.
So long ago we loved each other,
enchanted together by ideas and poems, stories
that have taken us our lives to understand.
Once in a candle-lit room
under the big trees in Memphis, Tennessee,
we decided that existentialism, like God, is dead,
one more story to add to all the other stories.

My grandson begins to cry. He cries so naturally.
He is tired and scared, hungry for his mother's milk.
I keep on walking.
Of course I am worried and think maybe

I should take my grandson back to his mother my daughter
so he can suck at her breasts, but I don't
because I really want to walk into the mountain.

I say out loud, "It's okay for a grandson to cry
if he's riding on his grandfather's back."

I say it again, "It's okay for a grandson to cry
if he's riding on his grandfather's back."

My heart, which has been blue all day,
wanders like the crow with the eye of the moon.
Strange moon. Strange heart.

Thank you, Crow.

Our many worlds are created by stories,
and we are little bits of human memory, seeds
afloat on streams of water rushing downhill after a rain,
water and earth, fire and sky, twisting and changing.
Now after all this time I can accept that, and I can say
this is my story, this is the place where I live,
and I will continue to write my story as I go along.

My grandson's crying becomes a sobbing, his way to tell me
he's tired, he's cold, he wants to go home to his mother.
"Soon," I whisper to him, "but not yet. Please not yet."

We leave the houses and the streets behind us.
We enter the flanks of the mountain.
The canyon walls begin to narrow.
Crow puts on the flesh of winter and begins whispering to me
like my lover who has been waiting,
glad that I've left my office of books and the computer screen.
The grasses are brown, the leaves are on the ground.
White-crowned sparrows twitter in the early darkness.
Startled dove flee up the sides of the canyon.
Crow lets the dark crawl down the mountain toward us.
and the night Crow brings is chilly and quiet.
My grandson isn't crying anymore.
I twist round just enough to see his large dark eyes.
He is watching the new stars sprouting,
the stars which are scattered seed.
Like we are scattered seed.
My grandson begins to giggle and wave his arms at the stars.
Then he goes to sleep.
We are riding the crow's back.
My grandson is sleeping.
Stones under my feet.
Millions of years of stones.

Thank you, Crow.

I turn round and pick my way down through the rocks
down through the flank of the mountain

and walk between the houses where families are getting ready for supper.
My mind goes off somewhere else, already back in my office
making plans about events that will never happen.
I come to the house where my grandson lives.
His mother who is my daughter is waiting for us.
She takes my grandson off my back.
She smiles at me.
And then she opens her blouse so she can feed her son.

The Art of Poetry

When I was a young poet I loved Philip Whalen's poems so much
That Philip Whalen became a hero in my heart.
My hero-poet went off and became a bald-headed Zen monk.
Years passed and then I heard
Philip Whalen read his poems in the flesh and the blood.
He didn't read his poems like I thought he should.
He didn't shout them with the holy energy that I thought they deserved
And he was surrounded by a reverent and hungry herd of dharma heirs.
They were like mollusks on the side of an old ship.
They were.
So I decided I didn't like Philip Whalen's poems so much after all.
His poems slipped into my darkness.
I went about writing my poems and trying to make a living.
More years passed like a mountain
Sitting quietly in the desert wanting to be a mountain again.
Then one morning I woke up and forgave Philip Whalen.
He could read his poems any way he wanted.
He could be a bald-headed Zen monk any way he wanted
Me, I was going to read his poems the way I wanted to
Because some of those poems
Are landmarks in the journey of my heart.

Ode for 60 Years on the Planet

FOR JOE SOMOZA

Hey, Joe,
I've decided I don't want to die.
Not yet.
I'm not ready.
So let's make a pact.
Let's not write any more about growing old.
Instead, let's install immortality into our poems.
We'll become famous that way.
Our grandchildren will remain perfect forever,
and our children will applaud our heroism,
even though they'll wink and roll their eyes
behind our celebrated backs.
Why, they will ask each other,
did those old farts want to live forever?
I for one will not be listening.
I will be adrift in my yellow Cadillac—
leather seats, the smell of money,
a wet bar, tinted windows bulletproofed.
I want to run away from home.
I don't know why I moved to El Paso anyway.
My life is speckled and soiled with mistakes and bravado.
A black man is my chauffeur.
He doesn't want to listen to my complaints.
His name is James.

He used to drive my grandfather around Memphis.
He makes me ride in the backseat.
The angels are fluttering overhead.
Their wings are idyllic, their voices perfect, their harps golden,
but they have no sex between their legs
and those fancy harps are innocent of mistakes—
thus, no jazz is allowed.

Oh well.

At least Fats Domino is playing his piano
and singing "Blueberry Hill". . .

   The moon stood still
   on Blueberry Hill
   And lingered until
   my dreams came true

I ask James if Fats has a yellow Cadillac.
James clicks his tongue and says something in Swahili.
He wants me to mind my own business.
I tell him that I want to discuss the poetics of immortality.
Maybe he can put me in touch with Fats.
James says my Swahili is not up to the task.
That's when you call me on my cell phone, Joe.
You and Jill are going away on a trip back east.
You have decided not to take any chances, thank God,
so you are taking your poetry along for the ride.

You get inside the Silver Saturn
Jill carefully hides your bag of poems under the front seat.

Your leaving makes me sad.
Then I see Lee through the tinted windows.
She is standing on the corner of Cotton and Montana.
She is waving goodbye.
"Paradise," she yells, "is like being lost
in the Museum of Natural History on Monday afternoon.
The guards are asleep, the bathrooms are locked.
It's good for a while, then everything gets old and dead.
Very old.
Very dead."

Lee wants to say something else but James steps on the gas.
He wants no truck with a white woman.

"But that's my wife," I say.

"So what?" James says. "My business is to drive the car.
Your business is to be the passenger.
The only passenger."
He smiles with those big teeth capped with the gold of my childhood.

"That's no good," I say, "I'd rather be dead."

James slams on the brakes.
The door opens.
I tell James goodbye and wish him well in the ether.

He kisses me goodbye on the lips.
A little bit of tongue.
He whispers something, but I don't understand.
He switches to perfect English.
"Yes," he says, "Swahili is useless in certain situations."
The angels have disappeared forever,
the hot desert wind is blowing,
and the sky is dirty with dust,
one of those miserable spring days in El Paso
where husbands and wives want to kill each other,
drivers are running each other off the road.
I walk inside my house.
Dust is creeping through the windows.
The plants are beginning to wilt.
Lee is waiting for me.
She tells me the plumbing is busted again,
our granddaughter is sick,
—pobrecita, we love her so much—
and we need money to pay our taxes.

"What will we do?"

We decide it's best to take a bath.
Lee, God bless her, has bought a bottle of Italian wine.
We light candles.
The sheets are fresh and clean.
We listen to Lena Horne sing songs about love and heartbreak.
We get drunk like young lovers.

Thirty-five years have passed since we first made love.
Her body has birthed our three children.
We do things to each other we've never done before.
And then it's over.
Our bodies are wrapped together like snakes sated with apples.
She gives me her lazy post-coital grin.
We know that death is gravity pulling at us,
that this energy is slowly seeping away.
But that's okay.
This is West Texas along the Rio Grande.
Mexico is on the other side.
We are learning not to ask for more.

Ode to My New Suspenders

This is what I've learned so far—

A man puts his suspenders on his pants,
then he puts on his pants,
and finally he puts on his belt
that is, if he wants to wear a belt.
I have decided not to wear a belt.

So today my pants hang from my shoulders
like wet pants hang from a clothes line to dry

                or, better

like when I was a little boy
and my family and the Christian earth
hung from the wide shoulders of God . . .

        before Camus and Darwin,
        the Buddha and the saintly physicists,
        even Jesus himself

began to create for my imagination
a holy model of the world
that breathes form rising up from seed,
disappearing again
into the muck,
Jacob's Ladder climbing nowhere

except into the end of self,
a Mobius strip of form and emptiness.

                    This is my plan—

from now on when I buy my pants
I will stop worrying so much about how big my waist is.
I will buy pants bigger round than I need,
and I will grow older each day
more happily,
my pants hanging from my shoulders
for no reasons of epistemology.

                    Yes, the wind

blowing against the desert willow in my backyard
will be sufficient reason for my existence,
likewise the seasons changing one to the next,
the earth a mote of dust spinning
through the wilderness of the universe

                    until one day

the seasons will quit changing the moods of my heart,
the doctors will scavenge my body
divvying up any usable parts,
and my children and wife will freely give away
all my shirts, pants, belts and suspenders
to the Salvation Army.

My Granddaughter Hannah

My granddaughter Hannah
Who has nine years
Her body beginning to sprout
Like a garden

In the first warm days of spring
Even though now
It's almost winter solstice
And I am an old man

Feeding the birds in the backyard
As a way to pay homage
To the earth and its countless beings
Oh my granddaughter Hannah

Who wears her thick sandy hair
Long
Like mountain streams
Running downhill

Oh my granddaughter Hannah
Who sits down in my house
And reads in a friend's book
His almost haiku poems

Trees and stones, wind and fire
Elemental bits and pieces of love
She says she likes poems okay
She says she likes stories about girls

She says she doesn't like boys
Not yet
She says the horse she rides
Well, his name is Cinnabar

How to Chop an Onion

This morning, chopping onions for beans, I remember my friend David teaching me how to slice and chop an onion, one of the little chores of mindfulness that keeps us sane and alive. We were working in the kitchen at the Radium Springs Hotel. He was the chef and I was the helper. He washed clean the cutting board and he sharpened his 12-inch chopping knife. German-made. High-grade steel. "Every chef," he said, "must have a knife like this." He grabbed a big yellow onion. He cut the ends off—the head and the tail. He brushed the debris aside for the compost. Then he turned the onion to the side and let the blade drop, cutting into several layers of onion. He turned the onion round and repeated. Then he peeled away the layers and brushed them aside for the compost. He had in his large hand the glistening white core of the onion.

Beginning to slice the onion, he told me to pay attention to his left hand. "See," he said, "I curve my fingertips underneath so I'm gripping the onion with my knuckles. That way I don't cut my digits off. Cool, huh? Cooks in a restaurant are always losing the tips of their fingers."

He blew on his fingertips like a safe-cracker and he smiled.

After he finished making perfect thin slices, he reformed the onion and started chopping it, his left hand above the point serving as the fulcrum, rocking the knife back and forth. The pieces of onion became smaller and smaller as he scraped them back into a pile and continued chopping.

A year after he taught me how to chop an onion, David bought himself a .22 gauge rifle. He was sad and lonely. He had quit his cooking. He drove to the Doña Ana dump and shot himself in the soft place under the ear. He disappeared forever.

Lao-Tzu and the Desert of Chihuahua

Scholars are not real sure when Lao-Tzu lived.
He might have been older than Confucius, that other Chinese guy.
They think he was a bureaucrat who looked after the archives
in some petty kingdom stuck out in the boondocks
where man-eating tigers still roamed the wild hills
and the farmers didn't even speak Chinese.
That place was so far from the Emperor's Palace it might have been El Paso.
The damn scholars are not even sure what the old man's name was.
Maybe it was Lao-Tzu. Maybe it wasn't.
Lao-Tzu, or whatever his name was, didn't really care what people called him,
so he left little trace of himself, except for this book I have in my hands.
I read it for the sixth time this morning.
I don't know if my life has changed or not because of this book.
I hope so.
It's afternoon now,
and an unexpected summer thunderstorm has climbed over the mountain,
the sky suddenly dark, lightening ripping at the fabric of clouds.
The earth is soaking up the first few drops of warm rain.
Soon I will go outside and get soaking wet.

Ode to the End of Summer

El Paso, Texas, 2005

When September
and then October
finally
arrive
on this border
between us and them,
and the last little dribbles
of monsoons
become old memories,
then summer
puts his big red violin
in its scroungy case,
he shows us
his fat buttocks
as he goes walking,
a dying god,
down the road.
He steals away the sunlight
as he wanders off
step after slow step,
the dust rising
and the cicadas crunching
under his big shoes.
Oh, those hummingbirds
in the leafy mulberry tree—
they have already forgotten

their daily hunger
and the lust
that brought them here
in the first place.
They are ready
to follow
fat hot summer—
they are ready
to leave me alone.

•

Like any other old man
I go to Albertson's twice a week
and sit at the blood pressure machine
peering at my death
through a magnifying glass.
The clerks look up at me,
and I worry that they see
the jangled necklace
of each year of my life
hanging around my neck
like cheap costume jewelry.

•

Take, for instance,
this lovely cool evening,
Orion's belt swirling
in the darkness—
I'm eating juicy

peaches with real cream,
and I'm thinking
that autumn carries her body
sexual and succulent
(she wants me for her lover)
her shoulders draped
with beautiful but
dying flowers, yes,
she knows the same secrets
my wife discovered
after menopause
carved an emptiness
in the holy place
where once
our three children lived.

•

Tomorrow is the Sabbath.
I plan to work in the yard
pulling at the Bermuda grass
that refuses to stay
where it belongs.
I will also dig a hole
in the backyard
for a mesquite tree
that will grow thick and bushy
under the hot desert sun
long after fire has turned
my body to ash.

What Happened on My Front Porch

Last night Allen Ginsberg waved goodbye
forever. Several bees, a scorpion and a butterfly
joined him in his departure, although I didn't
see them go off together. Their disappearance
was purely speculation. Before saying goodbye
Allen murmured that he doesn't believe
in a world of things. Why should he?
The end has never been the end,
and the universe is an open field of play,
a way of breathing. Here we don't know what
is going to happen one day to the next.
Except we will suffer. Except we will change.
Allen smiled and blessed me.
He doesn't want to be bothered anymore.
He was wearing his beard long again.
He seemed very much at peace.
I was sober. The moon
navigated in and out among the clouds.
I listened to the trains on Montana Street whistling
and I could hear my neighbors two houses down
drinking beer and singing and chattering
about nothing. None of us will ever
know how wise we are. Inside
the house my wife was asleep,
she who for over 35 years has studied
the human geography of who I am.
Allen had tied his boat to the juniper tree—

a light boat, with short oars—he climbed
aboard and sailed off into the nowhere,
happy to have saved us all.

A Thread of Ubiquitous Light

Sometimes
when I sit quiet in the morning I find
a thread of high pitched sound,
an unending hum that resides at home
inside my brain
beneath
the flutter of self-centered thoughts,
the white noise of cars going back and forth,
a train that lugs tanks and ordnance toward a killing field,
sparrows and house finches chirp at each other,
the pigeons flap their wings, the grackles
scream their plaints of hunger and anxious love.

The composer John Cage wrote somewhere
that this high-pitched buzz
inside our brains
is the squeal of our nervous system,
a silken thread that stretches
back through the door of our mothers' womb
where we were all surrounded
by liquid night

is where I first heard my father's voice
saw his face . . .

My mother is dead now.
Like my father is dead.
My mother's blues eyes are shut forever,

her breath stopped repeating its magical formula,
and her hand turned cold in mine.

Every day

like a spider in the corner of a room,
I unravel the thread of sound a little bit more
and with the same sacred material
my children and grandchildren do the same.

A Story about Marriage

Once upon a time
a long while ago
there was a man

who received all
blessings under the sun.
Yet, he missed

something essential:
there was no place
to practice his gifts.

So he asked God
for the blessing of death.
God gave to him a woman.

But other peoples
tell the same story
differently.

Once upon a time
a long while ago
there was a woman

who received all
blessings from the earth.
Yet, she also missed

something essential:
there was no place
to practice her gifts.

So she too asked God
for the blessing of death.
God gave to her a man.

Because of these stories
babies are now baptized
in their mother's blood.

And from these two stories
did wise Solomon first
create his eternal seal.

So many stories, my love,
quilted together,
are true and real, like

you and me, me
and you, we practice
our marriage

in this little bit of
time and space—apart,
together.

Amen.

Dokusan at the Bodhi Mandala

The Roshi is old and soft
Like a cream satin pillow
Some aunt brought home from Japan
With its tattered laces and frills.
The Roshi giggles.
He says, Don't believe in God
Until you've experienced God.
At least that's what I think he said.
His English is so lousy.
He says there are no answers
And then there are no questions.
He rings his bell
And he tells me goodbye.

P.S.

Steve,

I don't believe in Heaven,
but I hope you're there
among the flowers and the bumblebees, I hope
you've had a chance to chat with
Socrates and Plato, those old farts,
who (I believe) muddied your thoughts
for the last 15 or 20 years.
Forgive me.
The living shouldn't argue with the dead.
So I won't.
But I don't have much news.
Here in El Paso July has been so hot
my Buddhism, like a broken down car,
has quit working.
The hummingbirds don't care.
They insist upon their enlightenment.
Like the sparrows and the ants.
Even the stones are enlightened.
I don't know what my problem is.
At least it's twilight now.
Miraculous holy twilight.
Lee and I are on the front porch eating
sweet New Mexico cherries,
homemade cornbread
and her delicious split pea soup.

I miss you.
Love, Bobby

Some Notes on the Cover Image and the Poems

Cover Image by Lee Merrill Byrd: Lee writes, "I like to take photos, but only of people's faces, particularly the faces of my family, my kids and grandkids, and the faces of my neighbors. At some point, I started making photocopies of some of my favorite photos so that I could write on these copies. The writing was all from the Bible, my favorite book. As I would think of the person in the photo, I would consider the things that were happening in that person's life and the prayers that I had for them, and I would begin. As I worked, other scripture would come to mind, until I was sort of lost in the drawing and the verses. I covered this photo of Bobby with lots of verses from the *Song of Solomon*, especially those of the Shulamite praising the beauty of her husband and lover. In that photo also are the beginning verses from Isaiah 55. For me these are reflections of the delight he takes in life."

A Visit from the Archangel Gabriel: This is more or less a "found poem." I found all the information and much of the language (some exact phrasing) in the article "Videotape of Serbian Police Killing 6 Muslims from Srebrenica Grips Balkans" by Nicholas Wood, *The New York Times*, June 12, 2005.

The Day I Met Pancho Villa in the City of Angels: The Hajj, of course, is the annual pilgrimage to Mecca, a central duty of Muslims during their lifetime. In 2003 U.S. authorities feared that Muslim extremists would celebrate the last day with an attack. I was in Los Angeles, where the media was full of the threats. My friend David Romo had been reminding me that until the al-Qaeda attacks on the Twin Towers and the Pentagon on September 11, 2001, Pancho Villa had led the only attack against the continental United States when his army attacked Columbus, New Mexico, in 1917. Like Osama bin Laden, Villa lived in desert caves and even the famous Blackjack Pershing couldn't find him. For information on the massacre of women at Camargo I used Freidrich Katz' *The Life and Times of Pancho Villa* and Elena Poniatowska's essay in *Las Soldaderas*.

Life after 60: Judge Herb Cooper died in December, 2005, in El Paso. He was one of those men blessed by many close friends. At the funeral home, his buddy Spider

Lockhart told me, "Shit, this sucks." I wrote this poem down on one of the 3 x 5 note cards I carry around in my shirt pocket.

The Hospice Poems: In December 2002, our close friends Steve and Jane Sprague— the god parents of our children—traveled to China. They journeyed with Steve's fellow tai chi students and his tai chi teacher. Steve had been practicing tai chi for well over 20 years, and he longed to visit the birthplace of his discipline with his teacher as his guide. Steve was a very dedicated lawyer and a workaholic to boot, and, like always, he worked night and day to finish up his chores before he left for the trip. He was exhausted and sick when he got on the plane. In China he contracted bacterial meningitis. The clinics in the small town in China where Steve got sick did not have appropriate antibiotics, nor did they have the expertise to diagnose his illness. He sunk into a coma from which he never recovered. Steve died seven months later in his living room in Albuquerque with Jane, their daughter Edna, his mother, sister, brother and many friends attending him. Somebody had left a copy of Steven Mitchell's anthology of sacred poems, *The Enlightened Heart*, at Steve's bedside. Those poems became a welcome guide for me through Steve's illness, and various of the poems are referenced throughout my poems.

Jacob's ladder is a tree that grows out of the earth: The italicized portion beginning *"prisoners anally penetrated"* was cut and pasted from "Bush's Mr. Wrong, the Rise and Fall of Chalabi" by Evan Thomas and Mark Hosenball, *Newsweek* May 31, 2004.

Ode to the End of Summer: All the odes in this section, of course, are homage to the long skinny odes of Pablo Neruda. In his "Ode to Summer," Neruda has the season playing a red violin.

What Happened on My Front Porch: The last line is stolen from Philip Whalen's wonderful poem "Hymnus ad Patria Sinesis," a poem which I first read in 1963 sitting on the floor in the stacks of the library at the University of Arizona.

Dokusan at the Bodhi Mandala: I was in my 30s before I realized that the study of Zen required the practice of Zen. When I could, I traveled up to the Bodhi Mandala in Jemez Springs, NM, for sesshin. Twice a day the big bell would ring, and Joshu

Sasaki Roshi sat on his cushion waiting for his students. How to realize the Buddha, he would ask me, when riding a bicycle? Or sawing a piece of wood? He would laugh at my confusion, and he would act like he was riding a bicycle or sawing a piece of wood, giggling the whole time. Then he would ring his bell, and I would go back and sit on my cushion.

P.S.: Sometime in 2005 the German poet Stefan Hyner wrote to ask me to contribute a poem to his anthology in memory of the Italian poet and Stefan's close friend Franco Beltrametti. I wrote an earlier version of this poem for that occasion, but in putting this book together, my friend Steve became the addressee. The poem grew and changed some because of this decision, but Franco is still there lurking between the lines with his witty smile and playing among the syllables. He understands.

Acknowledgments

a bit of sanctuary, this sinking ship
oh, I adore the sinking ship

JB BRYAN "LETTING PASS"

These poems would not be inside a book if a number of friends, family members and fellow poets had not encouraged me. First, my son John Byrd moved back to El Paso and said he wanted to get his hands dirty in the family business, Cinco Puntos Press, and he jumped in with both feet. He insisted that Lee and I pay more attention to our lives as writers and to getting our work in front of people.

Likewise close friends fed my heart with talk and laughter that always pushed me down trails that lead to the imagination and the urge to create—essayist and historian David Romo who was a teacher for me about the city of El Paso; poets Joe Somoza, Jeff Bryan and Benjamin Saénz—their improvisational friendships create a space for me where it's an honor to be a poet; and storyteller Joe Hayes who listens to my personal histories and who sings with me the songs of my growing-up.

A trio of poets in Las Cruces—Connie Voisine, Sheila Black and Carmen Geminez-Rosello Smith—read and commented on a number of poems in this book in sporadic workshops. They let me in the door and happily and wisely commented on the poems, and Connie and Sheila read the manuscript and made suggestions as I was preparing it for publication.

Many thanks!

Bobby Byrd—poet, essayist and publisher—grew up in Memphis during the golden age of that city's music. In 1963 he went to Tucson where he attended the university. Since then he has lived in the American Southwest. In 1978 he and his wife— novelist Lee Merrill Byrd—moved to El Paso with their three children. The city and the border region have become their home. He and Lee are publishers of Cinco Puntos Press. In 2005 they received the Lannan Fellowship for Cultural Freedom.